AMERICA AT WAR

THE WAR OF 1812

12 THINGS TO KNOW

TRISTAN POEHLMANN

BLACK RABBIT BOOKS

Table of Contents

Trading ships were an important part of the US economy.

United States Becomes a *Major Trade Power*

1

The American Revolution against the British was won in 1783. The American colonies had gained many freedoms. One new freedom was trading goods. Trading made the United States a world power. Their ships sailed all over the world, buying and selling goods.

After the war, Great Britain lost control of resources and money. It no longer controlled trade with the American colonies. This loss threatened Great Britain's **status** as a nation. The British hoped the United States would fail. Then the British could regain power. Great Britain still controlled parts of Canada. From there, it would be easy to re-take their old territories.

Great Britain faced other problems. French leader Napoleon Bonaparte planned to build an **empire**.

He wanted to compete with Great Britain's power. In 1793, the British went to war with the French. They fought until 1802. But peace did not last long. In the spring of 1803, Great Britain went to war with France again.

The United States stayed **neutral** during those wars. Choosing a side in the wars would have limited trade. America was at peace and growing. The government cut back on the army and the navy. Fewer soldiers and war ships were needed.

20 Number of years Great Britain was at war with France.

US **merchants** traded freely with other nations.
• France and Great Britain were at war from 1793 to 1802. • Great Britain went to war with France again in 1803.

EMPEROR NAPOLEON Napoleon Bonaparte was a strong military leader. He overthrew the French government in 1799. He became the leader of France. But Napoleon wanted to rule all of Europe. For several years he controlled mainland Europe. But then, he lost an important battle. In 1815, Great Britain jailed him on a remote island.

US Sailors *Are Forced* into Service

2

The Royal Navy was the pride of Great Britain. More than 130,000 men worked on 900 ships. But the navy always needed more sailors.

Navy commanders hired gangs. The gangs found and forced people to join the navy. This was called impressment. The gangs also impressed sailors from merchant ships. The sailors rarely fought back. They were beaten if they did.

By 1805, navy commanders were desperate. They started raiding US merchant ships. Sometimes, they found British sailors working there. Eventually, they pressed American sailors into service too. Impressed sailors had to prove they were American. But that took time. Until then, they were forced to work for the British.

THINK ABOUT IT

Why do you think the British Royal Navy always needed more sailors? What might have caused this problem?

HMS Victory, *British Royal Navy ship*

US merchant ship owners became angry. They needed their sailors for their ships. They wanted the practice of impressment to end. They argued that it got in the way of free trade. The US government listened to their complaints. US leaders **negotiated** with Great Britain.

Great Britain offered a **treaty** agreement. The Royal Navy would not impress American sailors. But the United States had to make trade **concessions**. President Thomas Jefferson did not want to do that. He did not accept the treaty.

Jefferson thought impressment was a threat to American rights.

6,000 Number of US sailors impressed by the British in five years.

The British Royal Navy always needed more sailors. • British Navy commanders began pressing US sailors into service. • US merchant ship owners demanded an end to impressment.

Free Trade between Nations *Is Threatened*

3

The United States stayed neutral in the French and British wars. It did not take a side. It traded freely to both France and Great Britain.

Great Britain did not want the United States to stay neutral. US goods helped the French. By 1806, the British passed laws to limit trade with neutral nations. British Royal Navy ships blocked American ports. Ships could not unload their goods to trade. In response, France limited British trade. American merchants were angry. Their ships were often chased and bothered. They argued that free trade had been outlawed.

In 1807, the conflict exploded. British sailors left to work for the US Navy. But the British wanted them back. The British ship HMS *Leopard* clashed with American ship USS *Chesapeake*. The British wanted to search

Chesapeake for the sailors. But the captain would not let the British on board. In response, HMS *Leopard* fired on the other ship. The blast killed three US sailors. Eighteen more were injured.

The US government stopped all ships. Trade goods could not leave port. This **embargo** protected US ships and sailors. The British and French could not bother ships or capture and impress sailors. The embargo failed. It did not change British or French laws or opinions. Instead, the American market suffered. Merchants lost millions of dollars. They became angry with President Jefferson. The conflict between the United States and Great Britain deepened.

Bank notes used in the early 1800s when the embargo began.

$40 million Amount of money the United States lost in trade in 1808.

The United States stayed neutral in the wars between France and Great Britain. • Great Britain and France made laws to restrict trade with neutral nations. • The United States placed an embargo on all trade ships.

Both war and merchant ships usually had cannons for protection.

4 United States Invades *Native Nations*

Tension was high in the Ohio River valley. American settlers continued to invade Native people's homelands. A **confederacy** of American Indian nations joined forces to fight back. Their capital was Prophetstown in Indiana. It lay on the Tippecanoe River.

The confederacy was led by two Shawnee brothers, Tecumseh and Tenskwatawa. They allied 30 Native nations whose homelands surrounded the Great Lakes. The British government sent weapons to help arm the confederacy.

Rumors spread that the confederacy wanted to kill American colonizers. This was false. But Indiana Territory governor William Henry Harrison believed them. In the fall of 1811, he gathered an army. He marched to destroy Prophetstown.

The army arrived on November 6. Governor Harrison agreed to meet with Tenskwatawa the next day. But that

1,000 Number of soldiers Governor Harrison led to attack Prophetstown.

Governor Harrison wanted to destroy the confederacy. • The United States defeated the confederacy. • The United States declared war on Great Britain on June 18, 1812.

A painting shows Tenskwatawa leading Native forces during the Battle of Tippecanoe.

President James Madison

night, young Winnebago fighters attacked. The surprise fight grew into a battle that lasted for hours. The army drove the confederacy into retreat. Then they invaded Prophetstown. They found it nearly empty. Governor Harrison burned the town.

Many Americans were upset about the Battle of Tippecanoe. They blamed the British for arming the confederacy. In June 1812, President James Madison declared war on Great Britain.

TECUMSEH AND TENSKWATAWA Tenskwatawa was called the Prophet. Tecumseh brought 30 Native nations into a confederacy. The brothers allied with the British during the war. Native nations wanted the United States to stop invading. The confederacy fought to stay on their homelands.

Tecumseh

Tenskwatawa

United States Invades *Canada*

5

Leaders in the United States declared war on Great Britain over free trade. They also wanted more land. They targeted Canada. It was nearby and sparsely populated. It was also under British rule. The United States had tried to invade Canada several times in 1812. Each attempt failed. The British, Canadians, and many Native nations worked together. They fought off the invaders.

The Battles of Frenchtown took place in winter 1813. At this point, the United States was not doing well. They had recently lost Fort Detroit. Their soldiers needed to push north, toward Canada. On January 18, they were able to take Frenchtown.

The second fight was four days later. It was a disaster. The American troops were not prepared.

Shawnee fighters launched a counterattack. Many people were injured. They chased the US soldiers away. The next day, Frenchtown was raided. They took injured soldiers and burned the town. In the end, 900 US soldiers were killed or captured. It was the highest number of American deaths during the war.

In spring 1813, American ships sailed into York, Canada. The port capital of Ontario was not well defended. The British soldiers surrendered quickly. But they did not want to leave their supplies behind. They set their own fort on fire. The fort exploded. The blast killed or injured hundreds of US soldiers. The US army was furious. Many wanted revenge. Soldiers raided and burned York.

American prisoners were killed at the Second Battle of Frenchtown.

3 Number of times the United States tried to invade Canada in 1812.

The United States wanted to capture Canadian territory. • Canadians, the British, and Native nations fought as allies. • The United States defeated the British at the Battle of York.

American troops captured York, Canada, during the Battle of York.

War Erupts on the *High Seas*

6

Early in the war, the US Navy surprised everyone with their success. The British Royal Navy was the best in the world. They had 900 ships. The US Navy only had 17. Most were not ready for battle. US merchant ships volunteered to help. Some were privateers, or private ships. They sailed the ocean capturing British ships and taking cargo. But most privateers did not fight warships.

The USS *Constitution* was the most famous US warship. *Constitution* defeated four British ships in battle. It survived direct cannon fire from another ship. Sailors nicknamed it "Old Ironsides."

USS *Chesapeake* was another famous vessel. HMS *Leopard* fired on it in 1807. The attack upset Americans.

6 Number of well-armed warships in the US Navy in 1812.

The US Navy and the British Royal Navy were not evenly matched. • US privateers captured the enemy's merchant ships. • USS Constitution became an iconic American warship.

It was a first step toward the breakdown between the two countries.

Chesapeake was attacked again in 1813 by HMS *Shannon*. It took the *Shannon*'s crew only 15 minutes to capture *Chesapeake*. Captain James Lawrence of the *Chesapeake* suffered a deadly injury in the fight. As he was carried below deck, he called out to his sailors. He said, "Don't give up the ship!" But *Chesapeake* could not be saved. The British took it as a prize of war. Captain Lawrence's words lived on, though. "Don't give up the ship" is still a US Navy saying.

The boarding and taking of the USS Chesapeake.

Small boats tow the USS Constitution *in order to outpace British ships. The British never caught up.*

PRIVATEERS OR PIRATES?

Pirates sailed the seas in the 1800s. They captured any ship they could take. Some pirates killed sailors while others just stole goods. Privateering was different. Privateers had an agreement with the US government. They captured ships only from enemy nations. Privateering was legal. Pirating was not.

War Arrives on the *Great Lakes*

7

The Great Lakes were like a highway. Ships carried soldiers between Canada and the United States. The lakes gave easy access to North American land. Much of it was Native people's homelands. Tecumseh's confederacy of Indian nations still defended it. Great Britain controlled Lake Erie and Lake Ontario. Those were the scenes of major battles.

Presque Isle was in northeast Lake Erie. American ships were built there. Master Commandant Oliver Perry was in charge. His mission was to build a **squadron** of ships. But the waters around Presque Isle were patrolled by the British. It was a dangerous position.

By fall 1813, workers had built 10 ships to challenge the British. Perry prepared carefully for the fight. He laid sand on the deck of each ship. Sanded decks gave sailors better footing. They would not slip in puddles of water—or blood.

Master Commandant Oliver Perry

10,210 Number of miles (16,431 km) of coastline on the Great Lakes.

Soldiers used the Great Lakes to move between Canada and the United States. • The Battle of Lake Erie was fought on September 10, 1813. • The United States won control of the Great Lakes area.

On September 10, the new ships met on Lake Erie. The fighting was fierce. After two hours, Perry's ship was wrecked. Perry ordered the rest of the squadron to sail toward the British. The Americans' guns worked better at close range. The battle turned quickly. By afternoon, all six British ships surrendered.

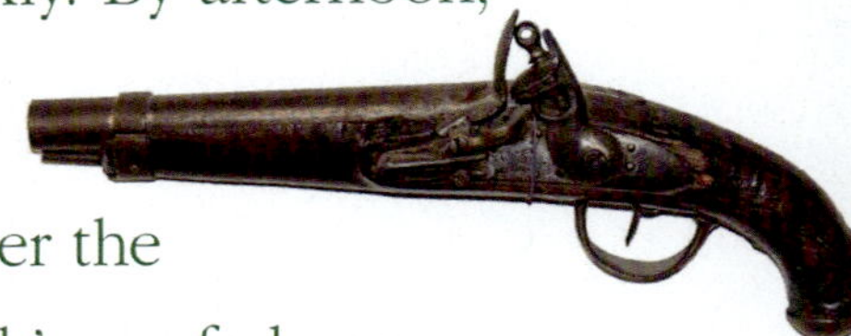

The United States had won control over the Great Lakes. The British and Tecumseh's confederacy had to retreat. The Battle of Lake Erie was a disaster for the confederacy of Native nations. Now, the United States had an opportunity to take over.

Tecumseh died in battle shortly after the United States took control of Lake Erie.

8

Washington, DC, Goes Up *in Flames*

Founded in 1791, Washington, DC, was a beacon of the new nation's freedom. In August 1814, the British took the city. They burned government buildings. They invaded the White House. It was seen as the lowest point in the war.

The attack on the city was a surprise. Twenty British war ships had sailed in months before. American leaders expected them to attack Baltimore. Instead, the soldiers landed near the capital. Washington was not prepared. The city had no defense plan.

On August 24, the British marched toward the capital. They had two missions. One was to distract the US Army. The other was revenge. American soldiers had burned the Canadian capital of York. The British planned to do the same. Some people fled the city. Others stayed to fight. But the citizens who remained were not well organized.

Statue of President Madison in Harrisonburg, Virginia

4,500 Number of British soldiers who marched on the US capital.

The British burned all government buildings except the Patent Office. • Enslaved White House servants saved many valuable items. • A servant named Paul Jennings saved a famous painting of George Washington.

The US Capitol building was still unfinished when the British set fire to most of the city.

There was confusion at the White House too. President Madison was not at home. His wife, Dolley, ordered valuables to be saved. Servants gathered important papers. The White House was empty when the British arrived. A group of soldiers lit the building on fire. Others tried to burn the Capitol. They blew up piles of weapons and gunpowder. The Library of Congress was damaged. Only one government building survived.

British Attack *Baltimore*

9 After burning Washington, DC, the British turned north. They planned to invade Baltimore, Maryland. Baltimore was the third largest city in the nation. It was a center of worldwide trade. Merchant ships in the harbor carried valuable cargo.

Baltimore expected the British. They had spent a year building defenses outside the city. They dug trenches at the base of a big hill. At its top, they built up walls. The trenches and walls would protect soldiers. They could fire at the British from a safe position. In September 1814, 4,500 British soldiers arrived. Army officers decided the hill was too difficult to attack. They left.

The Baltimore harbor was also prepared. A line of **barges** blocked its entrance. Each barge had two cannons. Fort McHenry was built on the river nearby. The fort was well defended. The British began a naval attack on September 13 at 6:30 a.m. They fired at the fort for more than 24 hours.

The **siege** of Fort McHenry inspired a poem. Composer Francis Scott Key turned the poem into a song. "The Star-Spangled Banner" would become the US national anthem. Key watched the battle from a British ship. At dawn, he saw that the US flag still waved over Fort McHenry. The British Navy retreated. The United States had won the Battle of Baltimore.

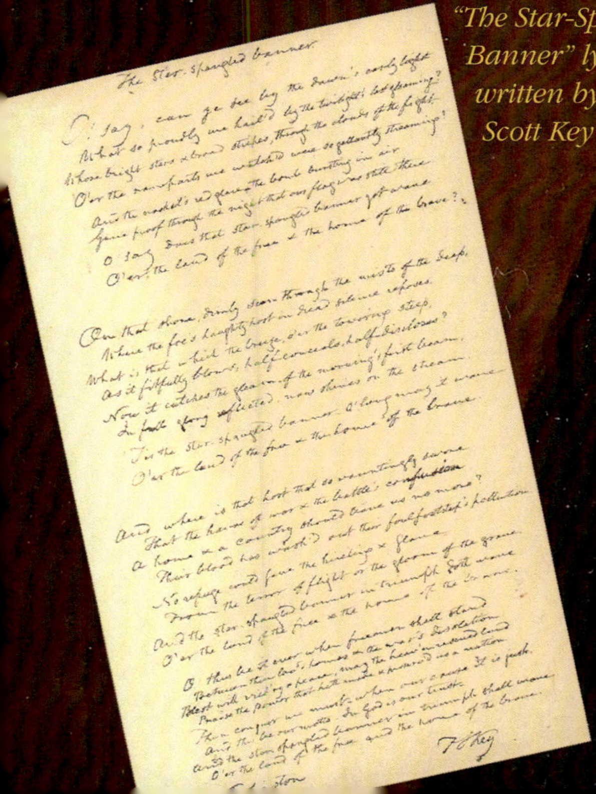

"The Star-Spangled Banner" lyrics written by Francis Scott Key (right)

THE ROCKETS' RED GLARE

Francis Scott Key saw Congreve rockets light up the sky. Congreve rockets were cheap, noisy, and easy to fire. They could blast over a battlefield or a war ship. They startled soldiers. But their aim was unpredictable. Sometimes they returned to hit the soldiers who had fired them.

1,800 Number of bombshells the British fired at Fort McHenry.

The British tried to invade Baltimore from two directions. • The British Royal Navy shot rockets from their ships. • The siege of Fort McHenry inspired "The Star-Spangled Banner."

Overhead view of Fort McHenry

Peace Treaty Signed on *Christmas Eve*

10

Peace talks between the nations began almost as soon as the war started. US leaders sent their peace terms to Great Britain in June 1812. The British rejected the terms. It took weeks to send messages across the Atlantic Ocean. Negotiations often stalled.

The final push for peace began in August 1814. American and British leaders met in Ghent, Belgium. The Canadian colonies and Tecumseh's confederacy were not represented. They had no voice in the peace talks. The British spoke for the Canadian colonies. No one spoke for any Native nation.

The Treaty of Ghent was made. It returned the United States and Great Britain to its pre-war positions. No land was gained. None of the original issues were solved either. The war had started over free trade and impressing sailors. The treaty did not address either issue. But the British

Signatures of the Treaty of Ghent

5 Number of weeks it took for a letter to cross the Atlantic Ocean.

Quicker communication might have ended the war sooner. • Peace talks began in Ghent, Belgium, in August 1814. • After the treaty, the British recognized the United States as its own nation.

Think About It Why do you think the confederacy of Indian nations was excluded from peace talks? What message did that send?

promised to stop supporting Indian nations. Now, invading Indian homelands would be less risky.

The treaty was a loss for the confederacy of Native nations. Their **alliance** with the British was broken. The United States promised to not invade their homelands. But without British backing, that promise was easily broken.

The Treaty of Ghent was signed on December 24, 1814. Officially, the war was over.

British (left) and American delegates meet to sign the Treaty of Ghent on Christmas Eve.

Americans Win Final Battle at *New Orleans*

11

While the treaty was being discussed, British leaders in North America planned to invade New Orleans. The city had access to the Mississippi River. Whoever controlled New Orleans would control river travel. But the British did not have enough boats. Land attacks were difficult and dangerous. The coast was covered in swamps, cypress groves, and thick brush.

US Major General Andrew Jackson ordered soldiers to block river travel. Cannons were put in place. Soldiers built **fortifications** outside the city. Walls were built out of sugar barrels and cotton

2,000 Number of British soldiers killed or injured in the Battle of New Orleans.

The US Army had about 4,000 soldiers. • They included civilians, Black men, and members of the Choctaw Nation. • The British attacked New Orleans for control of the Mississippi River. • News of the Treaty of Ghent had not reached New Orleans before the battle.

bales. Mud cemented everything together. Logs and ditches added security and cover.

British soldiers landed near the city in mid-December 1814. They attacked on January 8. But their charge quickly fell apart. The muddy ground slowed them down. Their supply lines could not move forward. Fog made it hard to see. Cannons fired into the fray. The army retreated. The navy could not reach New Orleans to help them. It was the worst defeat in British military history. The Mississippi River stayed under American control.

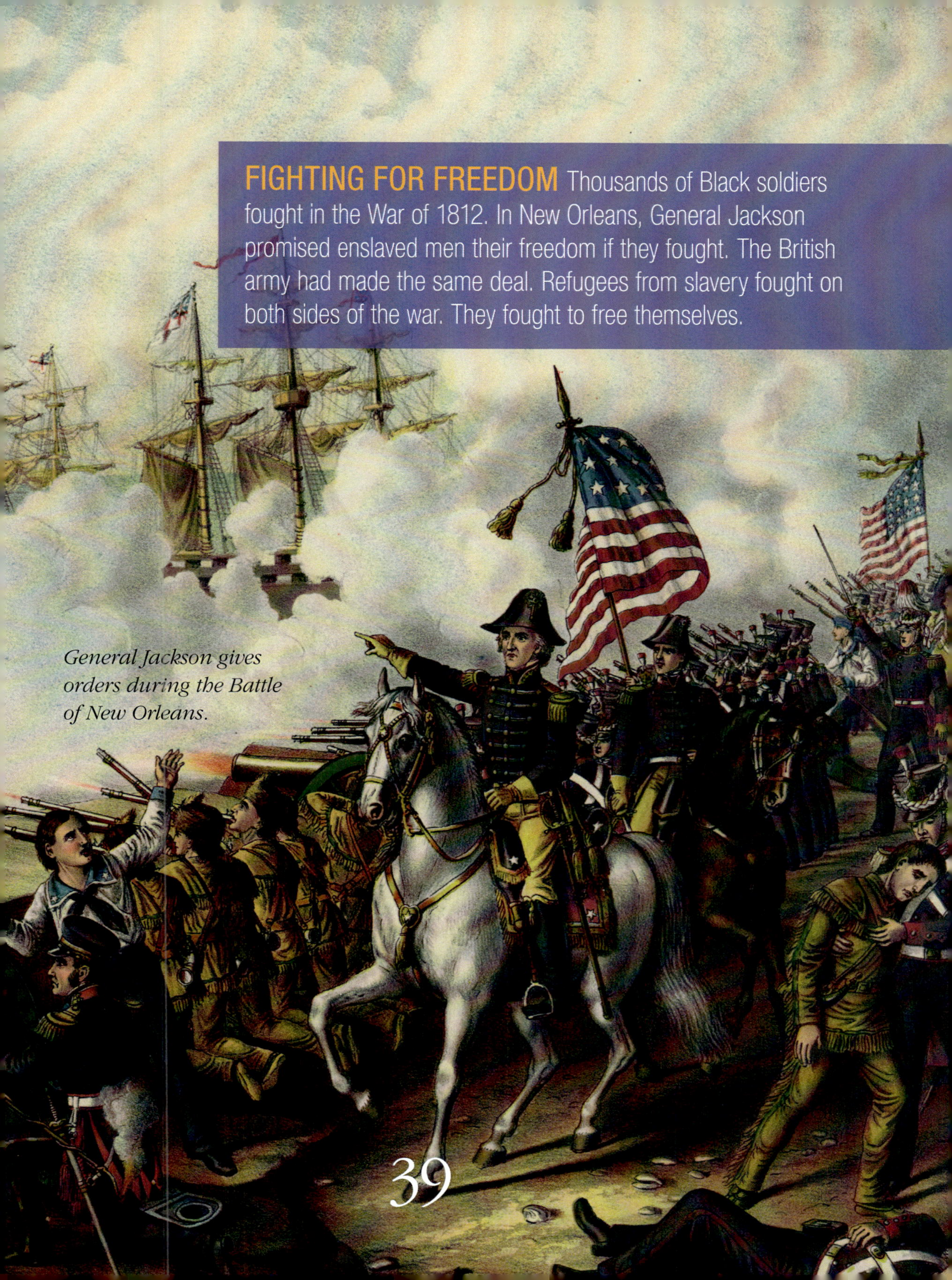

FIGHTING FOR FREEDOM Thousands of Black soldiers fought in the War of 1812. In New Orleans, General Jackson promised enslaved men their freedom if they fought. The British army had made the same deal. Refugees from slavery fought on both sides of the war. They fought to free themselves.

General Jackson gives orders during the Battle of New Orleans.

War's End Sets Up US *Land Takeover*

12

The US Congress approved the Treaty of Ghent in February 1815. Americans were proud to win their first war. **Patriotism** became an American value. "The Star-Spangled Banner" was the national anthem. The now-powerful government began a new push to take Native nations' homelands.

For many Native nations, the treaty led to their end. They lost British protection. More than 1 million American settlers poured onto their lands. The army forced Native people off the lands. Forced marches killed thousands of them. The US government called this Indian Removal.

The United States wanted to be a wealthy nation. Indian Removal was meant to help the American market. The stolen land turned

The Trail of Tears was the forced removal of more than 60,000 American Indians.

A statue shows a group of Chickasaw people as they arrive at their new territory.

into farms. More land meant more people were needed to work it. In the south, **plantation** owners forced enslaved people to farm cotton.

Both British and American leaders had promised to free enslaved Black soldiers. Most enslaved soldiers were betrayed. They were sent back into slavery.

The American market grew after the war. The cotton trade became important. Slavery made many slave owners wealthy. The United States became larger after Indian Removals. Settlers flooded west. The War of 1812 set up the shape of the nation.

Settlers move westward to new land after the Indian Removal.

Cotton became an important farm crop in the South.

12 Key Dates

June 22, 1807
British HMS *Leopard* fires on USS *Chesapeake*.

November 7, 1811
The Battle of Tippecanoe takes place in Indiana Territory.

June 18, 1812
President Madison signs a bill declaring war against Great Britain.

January 18–23, 1813
The Battles of Frenchtown take place in Michigan Territory.

April 27, 1813
Americans capture and burn York, the Canadian capital.

June 1, 1813
British Royal Navy wins a sea battle against USS *Chesapeake*.

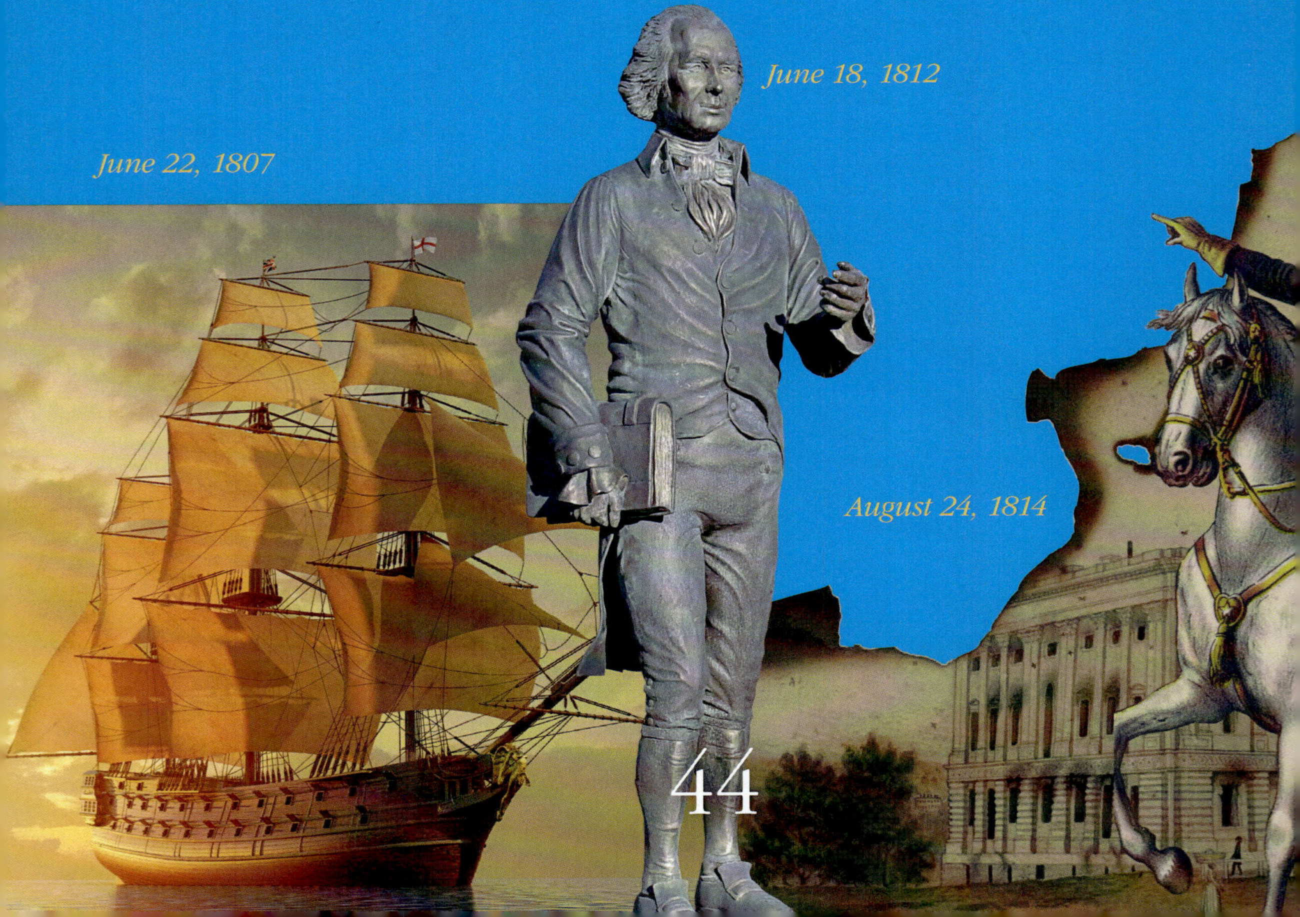

September 10, 1813
The United States wins the Battle of Lake Erie.

August 24, 1814
British capture and burn Washington, DC.

September 13–14, 1814
The United States successfully defends Baltimore.

December 24, 1814
The United States and Great Britain sign the Treaty of Ghent in Belgium.

January 8, 1815
The United States wins the Battle of New Orleans.

February 16, 1815
The US Congress approves the Treaty of Ghent, ending the war.

January 8, 1815

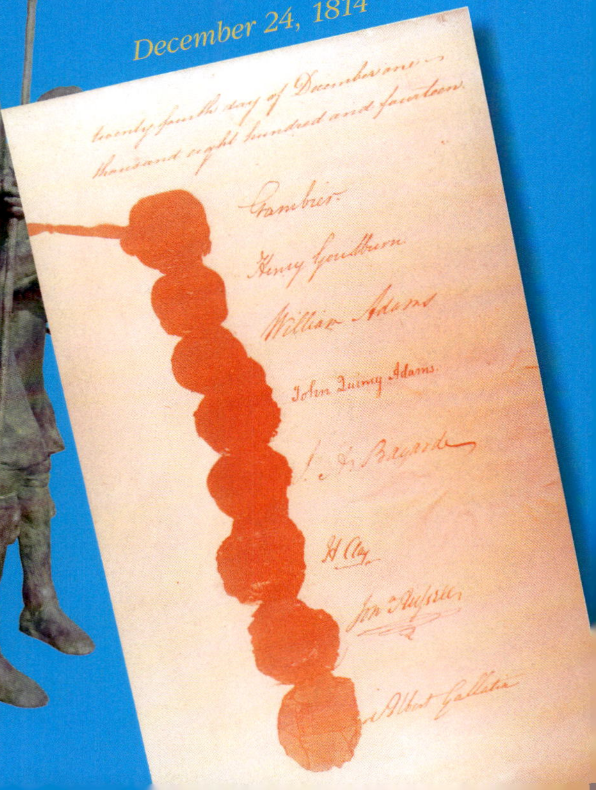

twenty fourth day of December one thousand eight hundred and fourteen

Gambier.
Henry Goulburn
William Adams
John Quincy Adams.
J. A. Bayard
H Clay
Jon. Russell
Albert Gallatin

December 24, 1814

Glossary

alliance
A relationship in which people agree to work together.

barge
A large boat with a flat bottom that carries goods on rivers and canals.

concession
Something that is granted or given up, often land or privileges.

confederacy
An alliance of people or groups.

embargo
A government order that keeps ships from moving in or out of a nation's ports.

empire
A group of countries or regions that are controlled by one ruler or government.

fortification
A wall, earth mound, or fort that protects and strengthens an army's position.

merchant
Used for trading goods.

negotiate
To discuss something formally in order to make an agreement.

neutral
Not supporting either side.

patriotism
Love that people feel for their country.

plantation
A large area of land where crops are grown and harvested.

siege
To surround a city and prevent movement in and out; usually includes military attacks.

squadron
A part of a naval fleet of ships.

status
Social or professional standing.

treaty
An official agreement between two or more countries or groups.

For More Information

Books

Doeden, Matt. *Taking a Stand During the War of 1812: An Interactive Look at History*. North Mankato, MN: You Choose, an imprint of Capstone, 2023.

Lombardo, Jennifer. *Tecumseh*. Buffalo, NY: Cavendish Square Publishing, 2025.

Ventura, Marne. *The Civil War: 12 Things to Know*. Mankato, MN: Black Rabbit Books, 2025.

Websites

Britannica Kids: War of 1812
kids.britannica.com/kids/article/War-of-1812/353909

History for Kids: War of 1812 Facts for Kids
historyforkids.org/war-of-1812-facts-for-kids/

National Parks Service: War of 1812
www.nps.gov/subjects/warof1812/for-kids.htm

About the Author

Tristan Poehlmann is a freelance writer of educational nonfiction. A museum exhibit developer for many years, he also holds a Master's Degree in writing for children and young adults from Vermont College of Fine Arts. He lives in the San Francisco Bay area.

Index

TOP RANK is published by Black Rabbit Books, P.O. Box 227, Mankato, MN, 56002. •

• Designed by Danny Nanos • Photographs © Alamy Stock Photo/Classic Image, 20, Prisma Archivo, 42, RP Photo, 18–19; Dreamstime/Georgios Kollidas, 25, Yalorik Aliaksei, 17; Getty Images/Greg Pease, 32–33; Shutterstock/Belinda Pretorius, 48, Everett Collection, cover, 1, fckncg, 8, ivanpavlisko, 7, JHVEPhoto, 17, Jim Vallee, 26, Jolygon, 46–47, MidoSemsem, 10, pdeminhiker, 37, Tony Baggett, 9, Vlastas, 13, 44, Vuang, 28–29, 44; Wikimedia Commons/Anton Otto Fischer, 23, Ben Schumin, 27, 44, Benson Lossing, 11, Blake, William O, 40, Captain Steele of the 2nd Battalion (British) Royal Marines., 30, Farmers Exchange Bank (Gloucester, R.I.), 12, George Catlin, 16, Harris & Ewing, 35, 45, John Vanderlyn, 16, Joseph Wood, 31, Kensett, Thomas; Tardieu, P. F. (Pierre François), 24, Kurz & Allison, 2, 38-39, 44–45, Kurtz & Allison, Popular Graphic Arts, 14–15, M. Dubourg / Naval History & Heritage Command, 22, Michael Bass-Deschenes, 43, Missouri History Museum, 24, Munger, George, 1781-1825, artist, 28–29, 44, N. Currier (Firm), 26, National Trails Office (US National Park Service), 41, 45, Owen Staples / Toronto Public Library, 16, Pearson Scott Foresman, 21, Public Domain, 31, Toronto Public Library, 34–35, 36, U.S. Navy photo/Released, 4, Unknown, 27, Volunteer Politics, 40

Library of Congress Cataloging-in-Publication Data: Names: Poehlmann, Tristan author | Title: The War of 1812: 12 things to know / by Tristan Poehlmann. | Description: Mankato, MN: Top Rank is an imprint of Black Rabbit Books, [2026] | Series: America at war | Includes bibliographical references and index. | Audience term: juvenile | Grades 4–6 | Ages 9–13 | Identifiers: LCCN 2024050101 | ISBN 9781644668573 (paperback) | ISBN 9781644668252 (library binding) | ISBN 9781644668894 (ebook) | Subjects: LCSH: United States—History—War of 1812—Miscellanea—Juvenile literature | Classification: LCC E364.9 .P64 2026 | DDC 973.5/2—dc23/eng/20241118 | LC record available at https://lccn.loc.gov/2024050101